PROJECT-BASED LEARNING IN SCIENCE™

EXPLORING FIELD INVESTIGATIONS

THROUGH SCIENCE RESEARCH PROJECTS

rosen publishing's
rosen central®
New York

KRISTINA LYN HEITKAMP

Published in 2019 by The Rosen Publishing Group, Inc.
29 East 21st Street, New York, NY 10010

First Edition

Library of Congress Cataloging-in-Publication Data

Names: Heitkamp, Kristina Lyn, author.
Title: Exploring field investigations through science research projects / Kristina Lyn Heitkamp.
Description: First edition. | New York : Rosen Central, 2019 | Series: Project-based learning in science | Audience: Grades 5–8. | Includes bibliographical references and index.
Identifiers: LCCN 2018009220| ISBN 9781508184751 (library bound) | ISBN 9781508184744 (pbk.)
Subjects: LCSH: Science—Methodology—Juvenile literature. | Research—Juvenile literature. | Science projects—Juvenile literature.
Classification: LCC Q175.2 .H4545 2018 | DDC 507.8—dc23
LC record available at https://lccn.loc.gov/2018009220

Manufactured in the United States of America

CONTENTS

INTRODUCTION

On a warm summer day in 2009, high school student Kevin Terris discovered Joe, the youngest and most complete duck-billed dinosaur fossil found to date. Kevin and his classmates were hunting for fossils in Utah's Grand Staircase Escalante National Monument. They were participating in a paleontology field investigation as part of a science class. Kevin hiked up along a ridge and found what looked like a bone fragment sticking out from underneath a mushroom-shaped rock called a hoodoo. He had discovered a string of toe bones, which led to finding the skull and later the skeleton of a baby *Parasaurolophus*. The area had been surveyed in previous years, even just a few days prior to their exploration. But it was Kevin's sharp eye that led to this important scientific discovery.

A field investigation is a scientific research process. It involves an organized collection of data from an environment or ecosystem that helps answer a question. Scientists observe or collect measurements of plants or animals in their natural habitat without altering their environment. Field research may include organism behavior

Kevin Terris discovered the toe bones of Joe while prospecting for fossils in southern Utah. Joe's skeleton weighed an estimated 1,000 pounds (454 kilograms) and was carried out by a helicopter.

studies or geological field studies, like the investigation in which Kevin found the dinosaur fossil.

Field investigations help to answer all sorts of questions. But the first step is to figure out the question. Good questions often come from being out in the field and observing the world around us. There are three types of questions in field investigations—descriptive, comparative, and correlative. Descriptive investigations ask questions that focus on measurable and observable variables, such as the number of living organisms in a specific area. Comparative questions pick more than one variable to investigate and compare, such as observing animal behavior during the day and at night. Correlative research involves observing or collecting data on two variables and looking for a pattern or relationship between the two, such as the correlation between sunlight and tree growth.

Once a question is selected, background research in needed to inform the investigation. If a scientist wants to discover what plants thrive in a riparian forest, she will first need to know how to identify different plant and tree species. After doing research, a hypothesis and investigation plan is formulated. Before heading out into the field, scientists know what data to observe and gather that will help inform their hypothesis. With science journal in hand, they step out into the field!

After following the steps in the planned field investigation, scientists apply gathered knowledge to their question. They look for patterns, analyze trends, and compare data. But answers aren't always straightforward and sometimes lead to more questions. If their question wasn't answered, scientists consider redesigning the project or reshaping their question. Then scientists find the best way to share the information. There are many ways to tell stories of science, either through bar graphs or pie charts or getting creative and making an animated video.

Unlike discovery in a science lab, field investigations inspire breakthroughs beyond four walls and fluorescent lights. Field research and project-based learning in science are like two peas in a pod. Project-based learning is a way to uncover knowledge by getting your hands dirty, asking small or big questions of the world, and stepping outside a science book or classroom to find answers. Project-based learning empowers students to observe and describe scientific concepts in the real world. All it takes is a little creativity, a lot of curiosity, and the drive to discover.

CHAPTER ONE

NATURE IN NUMBERS

Said to be among the most difficult subjects, physics is often seen as either a big yawn or an elusive science only understood by the likes of Stephen Hawking and Neil deGrasse Tyson. But in reality, you don't need to be a rocket scientist or wear a white lab coat to study physics.

Physics is the study of matter and energy—which is practically everything in the universe. The ancient Greeks, including Aristotle and Socrates, are touted as the founders of early physics, while Isaac Newton and Albert Einstein are the subject's modern heroes. Physics includes astronomy, chemistry, energy, and more.

The goal of physics is to better understand the universe around us, from the tiniest molecule to our entire solar system. Studying physics includes studying everything from light waves to chemical reactions. Physicists apply the scientific method in field investigations to test and confirm scientific laws of natural phenomena. They ask big questions, like how did the universe begin and why does the apple fall from a tree. Then they attempt to answer those questions by observing the world around us. Newton is said to have been out in the field when he first thought of his system of gravity. But physics also has many applied concepts beyond the theoretical, such as the development of sustainable energy and the study of chemical data collected from body farms that inform criminal forensics. Investigating with physics in everyday life teaches us to ask the right scientific questions.

TIPS & TRICKS

A science-writing journal is a notebook full of reports, drawings, observations, samples, and discoveries. The first rule of science journaling is never leave home or school without it. The second rule of science journaling is to always follow rule number one. Other tips include:

- Keep a pencil or pen with your journal.
- With every entry, include the date and time.
- Write down all observations.
- Don't be afraid to draw what you see. The sketches don't need to be totally accurate but should offer visual insight.
- Write down questions that come up. Later you can search for answers.
- Keep track of all variables observed. Whether you're investigating an animal or plant, take note of any and all elements.

QUESTION: WHAT FACTORS AFFECT GRAVITY?

Gravity is a constant. It is like the beloved family dog—always loyal, always present. Earth's gravity is the force that keeps us from floating off into space and what makes things fall, such as the table scraps that drop to the floor for dogs to eagerly gulp down. Gravity is dependent on both the mass of objects falling toward Earth and their distance from the ground. There are also several factors that act against gravity, such as air resistance, friction, and buoyancy.

Air resistance tells us why a feather slowly flutters to the ground, while an apple careens straight to Earth. Air resistance is a type of fric-

If a feather and rock are dropped at the same time, the rock will land first because there is more air resistance between the air and the feather.

tion, or a force that pushes against a moving or falling object. Shape and distance can increase or decrease the degree of air resistance. For example a balled-up piece of paper may fall more quickly than a paper airplane. In the fifteenth century, Leonardo da Vinci tinkered around, playing with air resistance and drafting his version of a parachute. Using a pyramid of wooden poles and sealed linen cloth, Leonardo's parachute was later tested and proved to be successful in slowing down gravity's pull.

Friction can be seen in land surfaces. For example, take a slope or rocky cliff. Friction helps sediment and soil hold up the surface. However, gravity wins the battle when a rockslide or landslide slips into action, pulling the soil down toward the center of Earth. Water can assist gravity, too, helping loosen up friction's grip on the land, and once again gravity wins.

Gravity is also affected in water. When an object is submerged in a lake or stream, the upward force is called a buoyant force. If the density of the object is greater than the density of the lake water, then the object's weight is greater than the buoyant force and it will sink. But if the object's weight or density is less than the water around it, gravity will pull the water down against the object, and that is what makes it float.

PROJECT
GRAVITY IS SUCH A DOWNER

We feel and resist gravity every day, from getting out of bed to playing catch. In this descriptive field investigation, you will find and describe examples of different factors that affect gravity.

- *With science journal in hand, step outside to the schoolyard, backyard, or park.*

- *Find an area to observe. Discover as many examples of friction, air resistance, or buoyancy as you can find. If you get stumped, change locations. Look for less obvious examples, such as a bird riding a thermal or a stick floating in a river.*
- *Write down every detail of the effects, from how long it took a leaf to fall, to the pattern it fell in.*
- *Now imagine you're an investigator interviewing gravity. Gravity just called, claiming that something is messing with it. You're in charge of the investigation. Using a Q&A format, ask gravity specific questions about how it was affected, and answer with details about what you observed.*
- *If you're unfamiliar with Q&A articles, research a few examples. After studying the format, write up your own Q&A article to share with others.*

QUESTION: HOW DO DIFFERENT GASES PRODUCE DIFFERENT SPECTRA OF LIGHT?

Like gravity, light is everywhere. Only a small portion of light is visible to the human eye. Light is essentially fast-traveling energy that exists all over the universe. Visible light is part of the big energy family of electromagnetic radiation. Other members include radio waves, microwaves, X-rays, and gamma rays. This range is called the electromagnetic spectrum. Visible light is just a portion of the light in the electromagnetic spectrum.

Different types of electromagnetic radiation have different wavelengths. Energy particles travel in a wave pattern that swings up and down, between high and low points. A wavelength is the distance between peaks. In the visible spectrum of light, wavelengths are arranged from the shortest to the longest. As light travels through a prism, the wavelengths separate into the colors of the rainbow. Violet is the shortest; the light in the middle is seen as green, and red is the longest.

The color of a wavelength is associated with temperature. Hot temperatures emit shorter wavelengths. A candle flame can

The spectrum of visible light includes a narrow band of light known as ROYGBIV, an acronym for the sequence of color: red, orange, yellow, green, blue, indigo, and violet.

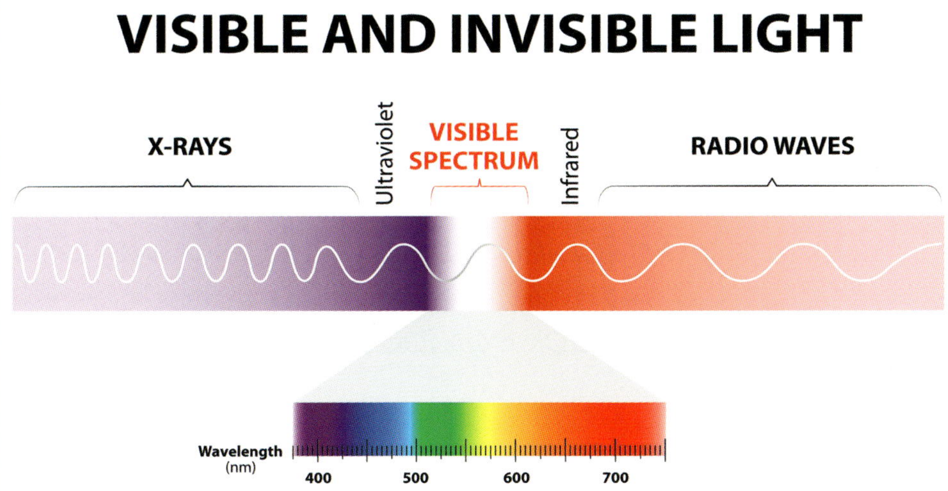

appear blue at its hottest point and yellow or red at the top of the flame. The sun's surface radiates a white or slightly yellow light. If the surface were cooler, it might look red. It would look blue if it were hotter. Astronomers study visible light to determine the chemical composition of distant objects in our universe, such as stars or space dust.

PROJECT
ON THE SAME WAVELENGTH

Scientists often bring tools into the field to help gather or collect data. In this comparative field investigation, you will build a tool to aid you in gathering visible information about the electromagnetic radiation of light waves. Spectroscopes are instruments that help scientists figure out the chemical makeup of different sources of light, such as the sun and the stars.

Materials needed:

- *Cardboard shipping tube or a paper towel roll*
- *DVD or CD*
- *Flat piece of black cardboard or card stock*
- *Tape*

Assemble:

- *Cut a slit at a 45-degree angle on one end of the cardboard tube. The DVD or CD will slip inside this cut and sit at an angle.*

- *Turn the tub over and cut a small rectangular viewing hole, opposite the DVD or CD slot.*
- *Trace the end on the cardboard or card stock. Cut out the circle. Snip out a rectangle in the middle of the circle. This is the entry point for the light source.*
- *Tape the circle to the top of the spectroscope (opposite end of the viewing hole).*

Investigate:

- *Aim your spectroscope at different sources of light (sunlight reflected off clouds, a wall outside, a candle flame, fluorescent light, or LEDs). Never look directly at the sun.*
- *Compare the spectrums of light. In your science journal. with colored pencils, sketch out the color bands that you observe.*
- *Like the bar codes on items purchased in the store, create color spectral bar codes for each light source. Invite your classmates to guess the source for each bar code.*

A candle flame emits several visible light spectrum colors, including blue, yellow, and white.

QUESTION: WHAT HAPPENS WHEN NEW MATERIALS ARE FORMED? WHAT STAYS THE SAME AND WHAT CHANGES?

Chemistry is physics' study partner. Both study matter and energy, but chemistry dives deep into the relationships between the two. Chemistry happens around us all the time. It describes the process by which a person's body chemically breaks down an almond butter and honey sandwich to extract the nutrients, giving it energy to skateboard home. Chemistry also explains life cycles in the environment.

Different chemical reactions, such as decomposition, are found in nature. Chemical reactions happen when atoms of substances are rearranged to form different substances. A decomposition reaction occurs when a chemical compound is broken down, or separated, into elements or simpler compounds. Decomposition usually involves an energy source, such as light or heat, to help break apart the compounds.

Fungi and bacteria help to break down dead or dying matter. For example, as dead leaves fall from trees they form a layer on the soil surface. Fungi, such as the mushrooms you see on the forest floor in later summer or fall, begin to feed on the dead leaves. The fungus grows and spreads from the nutrients it gets from the leaves, while breaking down the dead plant material. Earthworms and snails will also help break down the chemicals.

PROJECT
IT'S ALL CHEMISTRY

Decomposition happens in stages. All living things die. Or, more accurately, all living things transition into something else through chemical reactions. In this correlative field investigation, you will explore decomposition.

- *Search for a wooded area in your backyard, schoolyard, or community park. Search the ground for signs of decomposition, and select a specific spot. Place markers around the area, such as little flags, to ensure a consistent observing plot.*

A tree that has fallen and rested on the ground for many months or years is a wonderful place to find the stages of decomposition.

- *With your science journal in hand, identify what is decomposing and not, including organic matter such as plants and leaves and inorganic matter such as rocks or plastic.*
- *Describe what you see and smell, especially any life-form sprouting up in or around it. Record observations using drawings, measurements, and labeled diagrams.*
- *Observe over a period of time, ideally a few months, and note changes. Consider the elements that cause changes, such as sunlight or shade, temperature, and rainfall.*
- *Create a flowchart with the information observed.*

CHAPTER TWO

FROM PLANTS TO POLAR BEARS

Life is going on all around us, all the time. On your way to school, you may hear the shrill call of ravens chasing off predators or witness a squirrel gathering food. The study of life science concerns all that and much more. Life science studies living organisms, such as plants, animals, and even humans and their relationship to each other. Life sciences include ecology, botany, and zoology.

Gathering information firsthand in the field allows scientists to apply practical knowledge back at the lab. Sometimes scientists will enter the field in the hopes of gathering data to help formulate a research question. Or they may begin fieldwork with a planned question to study, but their question may change depending on evidence observed. The time Charles Darwin spent on the Galápagos Islands observing plant and animal life and collecting fossilized and living species aided in his groundbreaking theory of evolution. Life science explorations in the field can inspire critical thought and discovery.

Field investigations are used in several areas of life science. Scientists observe and collect data to develop a better scientific

H. J. Andrews Experimental Forest is a 16,000-acre (6,475-hectare) ecological research site in Oregon's Cascade Mountains. The experimental forest is world renowned for research and education in conservation management.

understanding of the natural world. This knowledge informs many areas of everyday life, from human health to environmental health. Or field research can help inform public policy. Field studies done in the H. J. Andrews Experimental Forest in Eugene, Oregon, pointed out the importance of old-growth forests to biodiversity. Because of that field research, forest management changed in the Pacific Northwest.

QUESTION: HOW DOES A SYSTEM OF LIVING AND NONLIVING THINGS OPERATE TO MEET THE NEEDS OF THE ORGANISMS IN AN ECOSYSTEM?

From a tiny flea to the dog it's living on, ecology is the scientific study of organisms and their interactions with the environment and other organisms. No matter how small or big, all organisms experience complex relationships with others just like them and with organisms of different species. These relationships can hurt or hinder each species. For example, the flea and dog have a parasitic relationship, which means that one organism is profiting to the detriment of the other. The flea sucks the blood of the dog, benefiting from the nourishment of its blood and the protection of its fur. But the dog suffers from the freeloader. The poor pooch gets itchy and irritated skin. In some cases, fleas can transmit other parasites, such as tapeworms.

Plants and animals may depend on each other and their environment for survival. Or they may compete for vital resources. This complex relationship is what causes organisms to change or evolve or to become extinct. Ivory-billed woodpeckers once made their homes in cypress swamps and mature forests, where they would feed on insects that lived in dead trees. But their population declined by the 1880s because of massive deforestation. The last confirmed sighting of this woodpecker was in 1944. However, some ornithologists, or people who study birds, are still hopeful that the ivory-billed woodpecker will be rediscovered during a field investigation.

Studying ecosystems usually begins with field observation. Thoughtfully walking through a forested area or quietly sitting on a beach, scientists take note of different players in the ecosystem and how they interact. After consideration and thought, they may come up with a question about the ecosystem. Then scientists collect data, such as vegetation surveys, to help inform their question.

PROJECT
SAVE THE TREES

An ecosystem is shaped by nonliving variables such as climate. In this correlative field investigation, you will explore your neighborhood or school and the variables that affect life there.

- *With your science journal in hand, identify areas in your neighborhood or schoolyard with a large population of trees. Also note areas where the tree population is sparse. Sketch a map of the location that you will be observing.*
- *Identify what species of trees are growing in the area. If you don't know, record a detailed description of the trees or take a photo. Investigate further on the internet or look for books in the library to verify the tree species.*
- *Record observations of the area. Then take a closer look at the surrounding ground area of each tree population. Identify variables that may affect tree growth. Are bugs living on the leaves? Record sunlight, rainfall, topographical location, and other trees or plants in the area that may be competition for resources.*

The best way to identify a tree is to examine its features, such as the shape and size, the leaves or needles, and the bark or flowering buds. Take the time to look closely.

- *Consider the relationship between the variables and the tree's characteristics, such as the leaf color and the number of sunny days in the fall. Is there a relation between two variables? Make a hypothesis about the relationship.*
- *With data gathered, create a map of the area with notes about different variables. Pretend you are meeting with an arborist, a*

person who specializes in the care of trees, to reveal your observation or notes about which tree species may thrive or barely survive in specific areas.

CITIZEN SCIENCE

You don't have to be a scientist to contribute scientific knowledge. Citizen science is the collaboration between citizens and scientists to increase opportunities for data collection that can lead to answering real-world questions. A popular citizen science project is the statewide bird count or identification with the Cornell Laboratory of Ornithology and the National Audubon Society. Snap photos or record audio and share gathered data with scientists working toward conservation projects. The online project allows citizen scientists to report real-time bird sightings and observations. Half a billion bird observations from around the world have been gathered so far.

QUESTION: IS THERE A DIFFERENCE BETWEEN MORNING AND AFTERNOON SOUNDSCAPES?

From the sounds of chattering classmates to the yip-yip bark of a neighbor's puppy, our daily lives are filled with sound. Soundscape ecology studies human, animal, and geophysical sounds. Human sounds, called anthropophony, include sounds produced by humans (such as talking) and sounds manufactured by human-made objects, like the roar of a plane overhead. Animal sounds are part of the biophony, which are sounds made by nonhuman organisms, such as crickets or birds. Nonbiological sounds from weather-related sources, such as the wind in the trees, the trickle of a mountain stream, and the rumbling sound of thunder are part of the geophony. Together, the anthropophony, biophony, and geophony create an environment's soundscape.

Soundscape ecologists look at all these sources of sound to determine the health of an ecosystem. These audio snapshots reveal important elements of an ecosystem that can't be seen, including the effects of climate change. Soundscapes inform scientists if an ecosystem is

A black-capped chickadee's birdsong is a simple two- or three-note whistle, but the tiny bird's song turns to a high-pitched alarm call when danger is detected.

thriving or not doing so well. More diversity of sound usually points to a healthy habitat. But unequal anthropophony noise can overshadow and disturb an ecosystem and its organisms.

The National Park Service (NPS) recognizes the inherent value of soundscapes as a natural resource that needs to be preserved and protected just as they work to keep the rivers, air, and soil clean in the parks. The NPS protects soundscapes for visitors and furry residents of the parks. A snowmobile's revving engine or the oppressive drone of an overhead helicopter can disrupt a visitor's experience or cause unneeded anxiety for the park's wildlife.

PROJECT
AN EAR FOR SCIENCE

Soundscapes can change over the course of a day, from season to season, and from location to location. In this comparative field investigation, you will carefully listen to a soundscape in your area.

- *Select an area in your schoolyard, neighborhood, or park.*
- *In your science journal, make three columns labeled with the different parts of a soundscape (anthropophony, biophony, and geophony).*
- *If possible, bring a recording device, such as a cell phone or hand-held recorder.*
- *Pick a morning time and afternoon time.*
- *For each day over the course of a week, step*

outside to the designated spot, and listen and record the sounds you hear. Closing your eyes can help focus your ears in on the different sounds.

- *Write down the different sounds heard in your journal with as much detail as possible.*
- *Compare the morning and afternoon soundscapes, and consider reasons for the differences.*
- *Using the data collected, create a presentation of your findings. If possible, include recorded sound bites and photos from each morning and afternoon observation.*

QUESTION: HOW DOES BIOLOGICAL SEX INFLUENCE BEHAVIOR IN ANIMALS?

Through field investigations, researchers gain firsthand knowledge they might not find in the lab or in books, such as witnessing animal behavior. Through detailed observations made during a long-term field investigation of wild chimpanzees in Tanzania, primatologist Jane Goodall discovered that chimps are omnivorous and that they make and use tools to hunt for food.

Animal behavior covers how animals interact with other organisms, either of the same species or different ones, and how they interact with the physical environment. Behavior can include how an animal hunts for food and how it socializes with others. Researchers observe everyday behaviors, but also pay attention when daily rituals are disrupted. Some behaviors are a response to ecological pressure. Innate or

Scientist Jane Goodall spent several years studying the behavior of chimpanzees in Gombe Park, Tanzania. Her work continues to inform researchers.

reflex behavior is an automatic response to ensure survival. If a turtle is poked, it will duck and take cover by retracting its head safely inside its protective shell.

Some behavior is learned. Animals will discover through observation, or through trial and error, how to interact with their environment and other species. A dog may develop an ear for the crinkling sound of a bag opening and associate the sound with tasty treats. Most animal behaviors are a mix of both innate and learned behaviors. A foal is born with the ability to walk, but it takes practice and patience for a young horse to fully learn how to walk and run. Behavioral ecologists observe animal behavior to help answer questions about the animal and its environment. Behavior is an important indicator of whether an animal survives, thrives, and reproduces.

PROJECT
SOCIAL GRACES

Different factors affect animal behavior, including biological sex. For example, female African topi antelopes aggressively compete for mates, while male topi antelopes remain elusive and almost passive. In the animal kingdom, some animals don't exhibit behaviors that researchers expect. In this comparative field investigation, you will uncover differences and similarities in behavior based on biological sex.

- *Select a species to observe. Make sure to pick one that you have access to and can observe both male and female examples of. Consider a domestic pet, such as a bird or fish. If you have access to goldfish or guppies, the fish's sex is fairly easy to identify by visual markings. If you're unsure how to identify the biological sex, consult a reliable source on the internet. Another option is to go to the local zoo.*
- *Without disturbing the animals or their habitat, observe and record behaviors of both the male and female. If the male and*

A local zoo or animal park provides a unique opportunity to observe, study, and learn from wild animals that we would not normally have access to otherwise.

female animals live in separate areas, try to arrange observation times around the same time of day.

- *Make a list of different behaviors, including what the animal does at rest, during play, and at feeding time, as well as how it grooms, or cleans, itself. Make note of differences and similarities in behavior. Consider the advantages and disadvantages of each behavior.*

- *With observation notes, create an ethogram to present to your class. An ethogram is a list of species-specific behaviors. The list describes in detail each behavior, such as what the animal does at rest, play, or feeding time. An ethogram is used as the foundation of animal behavioral studies. It can help to determine when a disruption happens based on usual behavior. An ethogram helps researchers compare and contrast the behavior of a species.*

CHAPTER THREE

DIGGING INTO KNOWLEDGE

The best way to discover new knowledge about Earth is to step outside and learn from it. Field investigations are essential to the study of earth and space science. Scientists have opportunities to observe and evaluate the dynamic systems, including the cycles of life on land, in the ocean, and in the atmosphere. Understanding the relationship between Earth and its systems and humans is vital to our survival. This knowledge provides us with a background that informs decisions in natural-resources management and helps us critically examine our impact on Earth. We have only one planet we can live on, and practically everything we depend on—our food, air, and water all come from Earth.

Field investigations allow scientists to learn about a phenomenon and then see it in real life. For example, a researcher may study the movement of tectonic plates and then step outside to observe how Earth's surface is constantly changing. Geologists spend a great deal of time outside in the field, studying and analyzing the materials that make up Earth. They observe and measure oceans expanding and shrinking, volcanoes erupting, or mountains eroding and moving. Geologists investigate natural processes such as earthquakes, floods, or landslides to better understand how they work and to prepare people to cope with these natural disasters in the future.

QUESTION: HOW IS THE WATER CYCLE AFFECTED IN AN ECOSYSTEM?

Nearly three-fourths of Earth's surface is covered in water. Water is not created but recycled over and over again. As water moves through the cycle, opportunities arise when it can be affected. As ice and snow on a cold mountaintop melt, water can become contaminated along its path down to a river. Mountain mining and metal waste can tip toxic elements into rivers. Agricultural pesticides can wash into rivers after a rainfall. Or as water is warmed by the sun and enters the atmosphere again through evaporation, other pollutants such as nitrogen oxides and sulfur dioxide can cause acid rain. When a contaminated river moves downstream, pollutants can seep into water used by humans, such as drinking water.

During the winter, snow collects on mountaintops. When warm weather comes, the snow melts and flows into rivers.

Hydrology is the study of the water cycle and its relationship with the environment. Hydrologists are water scientists who investigate water-related problems, such as how to prevent water pollution or how to find ways to control river flooding. A hydrologist may spend a considerable amount of time in the field, gathering water samples and data.

PROJECT
EVERY DROP COUNTS

A person can go without food for almost three weeks and survive. But a person can last only three or four days without water. Water is the most important resource on Earth. In this comparative field investigation, you will evaluate different sources of drinking water.

- *First, you will need to get your hands on three water testing kits. Water testing kits are available for purchase at just about any home improvement store, like Lowes or Ace Hardware. Most kits are under twenty dollars and test for things like lead or pesticides. Or you could contact your local water authorities. They might test a sample for free or recommend a laboratory that would be willing to test the water sources free of charge.*
- *Collect water samples from three different sources: tap water from your home or school, bottled water (any brand will suffice), and rainwater collected from a recent rain.*

- *Test all samples, and evaluate the different contaminants in each source. Note that some water municipalities add elements, such as fluoride.*
- *With information, create a bar graph showing the different levels of contamination found in each source. Present your information to the class, but withhold the source. Invite your classmates to guess which bar graph represents each water source.*

QUESTION: WHAT CHANGES AFFECT LANDFORMS?

While three-fourths of Earth is covered in water, the other one-fourth is, of course, land. There are many different kinds of landforms, such as tree-lined mountains, grassy plains, and the steep cliffs and deep valleys of a canyon. Our land has changed over time and continues to change. Weathering and erosion are dynamic natural processes that sculpt and shape Earth's features. When rocks are broken into pieces by tree roots or chemically dissolved by water, this is weathering. Erosion happens when those pieces of rock or soil are moved to another place by rain, wind, or water. Together weathering and erosion can transform Earth. A prime example is the Grand Canyon in Arizona.

Human activity also affects land formations. A forest once thick with trees and brimming with wildlife is now farmland. Shorelines are changing and even glaciers are shifting and melting. The human population continues to grow, so we need more land on which to build homes and produce food. As our land changes, so do the natural resources we depend on. Soil is an important natural resource

Different natural forces, such as weathering (by water, ice, and wind) and erosion, formed landforms like the Grand Canyon in Arizona and Arches National Park in Utah.

that plays a big role in food production as well as water storage and purification. Soil is made up of minerals from rocks, organic matter from plants and animals, and living organisms that call soil home. Soil supports life above and below Earth's surface. Without dirt, there wouldn't be life. Soil scientists spend time in the field gathering data, collecting samples, and studying how forces in nature and human activity change and affect the land.

PROJECT
FORCE OF NATURE

Examples of weathering and erosion can be found anywhere. In this correlative field investigation, you will be on the hunt for examples of both.

- *With your science journal in hand, find an area of erosion or weathering in your*

When observing during a field investigation, take note of everything you see, smell, and feel. If it's hard to put into words, try drawing a picture.

schoolyard, neighborhood, local park, or even your own backyard.

- *Observe the eroded area, and describe what you see. Take note of any variables that may encourage or discourage erosion.*
- *Observe the area over the course of a week (or longer) to witness a typical day in the life of the location. Try to pick the same time of day to observe.*
- *Note the animals and humans that frequent the area. Consider the different variables that affect the land, and take note of each. These will likely include water, wind, and human activity.*

WILL WORK FOR TREES

Environmental consulting is a popular job in Canada. Over 17 percent of Canada's environmental workforce works for environmental consulting companies. Environmental consultants help private industry and governments discover ways to lower their environmental impact. Consultants conduct field investigations as well as in-office research. They help companies lower their greenhouse gas emissions and employ safe waste-management policies. Consultants also perform environmental audits of daily practices to find opportunities for efficiency and sustainability. Or if a business is looking to build on new land, an environmental consultant will conduct field investigations and collect data to reveal if the construction and business would hurt the ecosystem.

- *With information gathered, draw a comic strip with your data. The comic should have a beginning, middle, and end. The beginning would show the area on day one of your observation. The middle would show the biggest players or sources of weathering and erosion, whether it's the family dog that likes to frequent the area, tree roots disrupting the ground, or water that gathers in the area after a rainfall. In the final sections of the comic strip, imagine what the land would look like ten years from now.*

QUESTION: HOW DO HUMAN ACTIVITIES AFFECT LAND, VEGETATION, STREAMS, AND AIR?

Since the Industrial Revolution, human activities in industry and agriculture have impacted our environment. Machine-powered innovation and mass food production changed our relationship with the land, air, and water. Life got a lot easier for humans but a lot harder for the planet that supports all life, including human life.

Human activities can interfere with the planet's cycles. The carbon cycle is the natural process by which carbon dioxide moves through the environment. Normally the cycle maintains a good balance of carbon. However, human activities have set the system out of whack. Burning fossil fuels is a major disruptor of the carbon cycle. When oil or coal is burned, whether to generate electricity in power plants or to fuel a summer road trip, carbon dioxide is released into the atmosphere, where it builds up. Increasing carbon dioxide in the air causes higher global temperatures. The land heats up and increases the decomposition in soil, and this too increases carbon in the air, much faster than the normal process. Another human activity that throws a wrench in the cycle is land use. When large swaths of forest are permanently removed and not replanted, it increases levels of carbon dioxide in the atmosphere. Trees capture carbon dioxide from the atmosphere though photosynthesis. Forests are often called carbon sinks, which means that they absorb more carbon than they release in the form of carbon dioxide. Clearing trees for industry or agriculture also mean the carbon stored in soil is released into the atmosphere.

PROJECT
KICK THE HABIT

Human activity continues to increase the amount of carbon dioxide in our atmosphere. But everyone can help out by decreasing his or her carbon footprint. In this descriptive field investigation, you will be observing your own habits and behavior.

- *Search for a free online carbon footprint calculator from a reliable source, such as the Nature Conservancy.*
- *Spend at least a week, ideally a full month, keeping track of the following:*
  - *Vehicle mileage: any time you get in the car with your family, ask to set the odometer to track how many miles your family drives. If you take public transportation, calculate the miles by using a map tool found online, such as Google Maps.*

According to the US Department of Transportation, the average American drives over 13,000 miles (29,000 kilometers) each year, which could amount to 60 tons (54 tonnes) of carbon dioxide released into the environment.

- *Ask a parent or guardian for this next calculation. Find the monthly bill for your family's electricity, gas, and water usage. How much is spent each month?*
- *Keep track of your diet for a week. Do you eat a lot of red meat or is your diet full of vegetables? Take note of how much you eat of each food category.*
- *Finally, keep track of your shopping. How much money do you spend on clothes, entertainment, or books every month?*

- *After gathering all your data, plug it into the carbon footprint calculator. The tool will offer you results from your data. Create a pie chart using the data. Consider ways to reduce your carbon footprint.*

CHAPTER FOUR

DESIGN BY NATURE

At first, it might seem like a stretch to put engineering design and field investigation in the same sentence. But field research is an important step in the engineering design process. There are several steps in the process of engineering design. First, identify a problem, such as how to create a safe way for wind turbines and winged animals to coexist. Next, brainstorm solutions. Keep in mind the available resources and constraints. Once a design is made, test the prototype. Evaluate the design and efficacy of the solution. If needed, redesign for limits or constraints.

Throughout history, humans have turned to nature for solutions to difficult problems. Nature has a lot to offer, especially designs. Following its lead, designers have hacked ideas from nature. Stealing design solutions from nature makes sense because the environment is like one big engineering design project. Through evolution and natural selection, organisms have faced problems and had to figure out solutions. Working within a set of constraints and environmental pressure, and over millions of generations, plants and animals have become their best selves or have found a solution to the problems they faced.

Climate change is already forcing several animals to find solutions in order to survive. The tawny owls of Finland are an example of microevolution, which is when a species changes over a short period of time. The medium-sized owls are different colors, either brown or pale gray. Pale gray tawny birds thrive during winter because their coloring helps them blend in with the snow, hiding them from predators. But because winters are now milder, there is

The yellow half circles in this drawing represent the biological sonar of bats, which helps them navigate when flying and hunting prey. The red half circles show how sounds reflect off surrounding objects.

less snow. Brown tawny owls are now thriving and passing on their genetics, changing the species.

Scientists and engineers have sourced some of their best ideas from biological evolution. Bats' echolocation, which allows them to navigate, inspired the development of submarine sonar. Clothing designers take inspiration from the plant and insect world to create waterproof materials. No doubt, we will continue to pilfer design ideas from nature as we plan ways to mitigate our impact on Earth.

QUESTION: HOW DOES NATURE SOLVE A PROBLEM?

Imagine learning how to use wind energy from a humpback whale. Or looking to lotus plants for the best way to keep kitchen counters spotless. Finding sustainable design solutions inspired by nature is called biomimicry. It's used everywhere, from architecture to medicine. Biomimicry explores ways to work with Earth instead of against it.

One example of biomimicry is the invention of Velcro. In 1948, a Swiss engineer and his dog went hiking in the woods, and upon their return the engineer noticed that his hound was covered in burdock burrs. He examined the burr under a microscope and discovered how it uses tiny hooks to grab on clothes or fur. Years of research and design later, the engineer presented his prototype. Soon, the National Aeronautics and Space Administration (NASA) was using the product. The Apollo astronauts would use Velcro to strap down devices during space travel.

A Japanese train engineer and bird-watcher looked to the beaks of kingfishers for design inspiration. Kingfishers have long and narrow beaks that allow them to quietly dive into water to catch fish. Engineers redesigned the high-speed bullet train with a quieter and sleeker design.

An adult male common kingfisher dives to catch fish. The streamlined shape of its body and beak helps the bird to break the water surface with hardly a splash.

Living and nonliving organisms, from birds to burrs, in the natural world can inspire new designs. Engineers can mimic nature or follow its lead. They find inspiration in ecosystems to better design communities and cities. Engineers also look to nature for what works and what doesn't work. Nature has already solved Earth's problems through evolution and billions of years of trial and error.

A DESIGN CHALLENGE

Every year, NASA offers design challenges and competitions. The opportunities invite students from kindergarten to college to design or build solutions to real-world problems. The NASA Ames Space Settlement annual contest calls students to design a space settlement. As permanent communities in orbit, these settlements must support life for an extended time, instead of just a month or two, like space stations. A permanent community would involve structures that millions of people, animals, and plants could comfortably survive and thrive in. Grade levels are judged separately. The grand prize winners are invited to present their design at the International Space Development Conference and receive a cash award. All participants get an official NASA certificate.

PROJECT
WHAT WOULD NATURE DO?

Everywhere you look in the natural world, you will discover examples of plants, animals, and ecosystems that came up against a challenge and navigated their way toward a solution and success. In this descriptive field investigation, you will take the lead from nature.

- *Begin your investigation online. The Biomimicry Institute offers a comprehensive collection of all things inspired by nature. Their AskNature collection offers articles, videos, and more to introduce the ideas behind biomimicry. Take some time to browse the site, and find examples of nature-inspired problems solvers.*

- *Next, sit down and brainstorm current design challenges in your own life. Big or small, write down design problems you would like to find solutions for.*
- *With your science journal in hand, step outside. Walk around and look for inspiration. Find examples in nature where evolution or design has fixed a problem. Write down any and all examples. Search for answers to your own design problems.*
- *Find the nature-inspired solution to your problem, and brainstorm ways to make it happen. Draw a prototype of your design*

Discover nature-inspired design solutions by sitting down and intently observing and recording nature and the environment. Be creative and think outside the box.

solution. Write a description explaining how your product works. Share with friends or classmates who may also have the same problem.

QUESTION: HOW MUST ENGINEERS TAKE NATURE INTO ACCOUNT IN THEIR DESIGNS?

Sometimes design choices are a matter of life or death. Thousands of birds and bats are killed each year by wind turbines in the United States. Fatalities include protected species, such as the golden eagle and the Indiana bat. Although fossil-fuels plants, pesticides, and even buildings kill millions of bird and bats, too, wind power is a growing industry. It's important for engineers of wind industries to consider redesign options to protect wildlife.

Bats play an important role in agriculture. Bats eat a ton of insects that help farmers save billions of dollars in pest control. While the rotating blades of a turbine slaughter bats and birds alike, bats are also killed by the rapid decrease in air pressure around the turbine. During a field investigation, researchers collected dead bats around turbines and discovered many bodies showed zero external injuries. After further analysis, researchers found that the lower air pressure caused the blood vessels in their lungs to burst, drowning them in their own blood. Engineers are tackling the problem by designing ultrasonic "boom boxes" that radiate high-frequency sounds in hopes of deterring bats from the dangerous air space. Other engineers are exploring redesigning the wingspan of turbines or using completely new designs that are much different from traditional designs, such as a helium-filled floating wind turbine or a bladeless wind energy generator. Whether it's saving winged animals or helping farmers, field investigations can inform and guide engineer design.

PROJECT
LOCATION, LOCATION, LOCATION

When designing a foundation for a project, engineers must perform a site investigation of the physical properties, a soil exploration, and a look at the habitats that may be impacted by the build. In this comparative field investigation, you will conduct a survey for a new build.

- *With your science journal in hand, walk around your neighborhood. You're scouting for a location for a solar and wind energy project.*
- *Spend at least a week searching to determine the best location for generating both solar and wind energy.*
- *Consider what elements are needed to produce the energies, as well as how the environment of the location might be affected by the build. Make note of wildlife in the area and other factors.*
- *Conduct research online to understand how much it would cost to build and how much money would be saved using renewable energy. Determine what type of equipment is needed and what is involved in installing solar panels and wind turbines.*
- *With data collected, develop a proposal that investors would read to consider funding the project. Include the location of the site, why it works best, the wildlife to consider, and the*

cost of the project. Don't forget to highlight the benefits of renewable energy.

QUESTION: WHAT IS THE RELATIONSHIP BETWEEN DESIGN AND HABITAT?

A habitat is where an animal or plant lives. It is its natural environment in which it either thrives or barely survives. A habitat includes food, shelter, water, and space for the plant or animal to live, whether it's resting, growing, or playing. An organism's survival is dependent on these factors.

All living things have a habitat, although not all habitats are the same. A freshwater fish such as a trout couldn't survive in a shark's saltwater habitat, and vice versa. An artic polar bear would have a hard time surviving in a black bear's habitat. Polar bears are the most carnivorous member of the bear family, eating large servings of meat

Polar bears and black bears are each adapted to their habitats. A male black bear weighs an average of 150 to 300 pounds (68–158 kg), whereas a male arctic polar bear weighs an average of 900 to 1,600 pounds (408–725 kg).

and fat from seals, whales, and walruses. But black bears are omnivorous. They gorge on fish, plants, berries, insects, and nuts.

But not all habitats are created equal. Some habitats are overcrowded and there is competition for space, food, and even mates. Animals can become aggressive and territorial over the limited resources. Overpopulated habitats also wreak havoc on the ecosystem and land.

When designing a zoo or aquarium habitat for an animal, designers try to mimic the animal's natural environment. The exhibit design incorporates all factors important to habitat, including plants, landscape features, climate, and anything to help the animal live a healthy and happy life. Research has shown that when zoo animals act out or misbehave, it's because they don't get enough exercise or their habitat is inhospitable. Zoos have experimented with giving species more options inside their habitat, like the ability to search for and catch their food.

PROJECT
MODEL HOME

Observing animals in their habitats, whether natural or human made, can inform design decisions. In this correlative field investigation, you will be on the lookout for what works and what doesn't in an animal's habitat.

- *Select an animal habitat that you have access to and can easily observe over the course of a week or longer, such as a fish tank or other family pet's domain.*

The quest for knowledge begins with curiosity. Scientific discoveries are the results of serious observations.

- *In your science journal, record how the animal interacts with its habitat. Are there areas that it frequents most? Does your cat like the sunny spot by the window, or does the goldfish hang out near the mossy plants?*
- *Form a hypothesis based upon this collected data. Why does the animal frequent that area of the habitat as opposed to another area?*
- *Design the perfect habitat for the animal based on recorded observations. Include details that highlight important factors of a habitat, such as food, shelter, and space.*
- *Create a brochure of the habitat designed for those looking for the perfect place to live. Include a map of the space and its special features, such as a climbing wall for the cat that likes to claw the couch.*

USEFUL TOOLS

The internet has many resources that could prove helpful for project-based learning projects. While it's also worth asking a librarian for ideas, here are a few sites with information related to the projects in this book:

- Learn more about creating and using an ethogram in this video lecture: https://www.youtube.com/watch?v=FtYX-aMQ4Qg. Produced by the University of Florida, Dr. Chris Mortensen offers tips on observation and how to design an ethogram.
- The Biomimicry Institute offers a comprehensive online tool called AskNature. It's packed with books, articles, videos, lesson plans, training programs, and more. Find it at: https://asknature.org.
- Looking for a good example of a Q&A article? Check out this interview with textbook author Peter Atkins: https://www.nature.com/articles/463612a.
- Need help making a spectroscope? Follow this written guide or video demonstration: https://www.exploratorium.edu/snacks/cd-spectroscope.
- Curious to see what decomposition looks like over a long period of time? Check out the University of Wyoming's video: https://www.youtube.com/watch?v=GzH_FVgE3C8.
- Learn more about water testing with the Environmental Protection Agency's (EPA) Home Drinking Water Testing Fact Sheet: https://www.epa.gov/ground-water-and-drinking-water.
- If you need help identifying the biological sex of your goldfish, read this article for tips: https://pets.thenest.com/goldfish-gender-identification-4191.html.
- Discover free online presentations tools at: https://mytechdecisions.com/unified-communications/15-online-tools-students-teachers-create-presentations.

- Listen and interact with soundscape ecologist Bernie Krause's great animal orchestra: http://www.legrandorchestredesanimaux.com/en.
- Learn more about the carbon cycle in this video: https://www.youtube.com/watch?v=r75NL3gN5yU.
- Learn more about how to calculate and reduce your carbon footprint: https://climatekids.nasa.gov/review/how-to-help.
- Explore the different steps in building a prototype: http://pbskids.org/designsquad/parentseducators/lesson-plans/structures.html.
- Want to build a prototype of your design project? Check out a Fab Lab near you: http://usfln.org.
- Easily create a six-page booklet for your brochure using this video: https://www.youtube.com/watch?v=WSjyJo8h7qs.
- Follow these seven easy steps to create a comic strip: http://www.mykidsadventures.com/create-comic-strip-kids.
- This article is the ultimate flowchart guide. Included are tips on how to draw a flowchart and templates: https://creately.com/blog/diagrams/flowchart-guide-flowchart-tutorial.

GLOSSARY

buoyant force The upward force on an object submerged in water.

carbon footprint The amount of carbon dioxide a single person or business produces through different activities, such as driving.

decomposition A chemical reaction when chemical compounds are broken down into simpler elements.

deforestation The clearing of a large area of trees for buildings, farms, or ranches.

ecology The study of how organisms interact with the environment.

ecosystem An area where plants and animals live and interact with each other and their environment.

ethogram A list of animal-specific behaviors, such as hunting or sleeping.

habitat A place where an animal or plant lives, including their food and shelter.

innate behavior An animal's automatic response to ensure survival.

learned behavior A behavior learned by observation, such as a bird learning to fly.

microevolution When a plant or animal genetically changes over a short period of time.

organism A living plant, animal, fungus, or bacteria.

parasitic relationship When one organism is benefiting to the detriment of another species.

photosynthesis When plants use sunlight to convert carbon dioxide and water into nutrients.

prototype An original or first model of a project design that is revised and further developed.

riparian forest A forest or wooded area near a body of water, such as a river or a lake.

spectroscope A tool used to figure out the chemical makeup of different sources of light.

FOR MORE INFORMATION

Association of Fish & Wildlife Agencies
1100 First Street NE, Suite 825
Washington, DC 20002
(202) 838-3474
Website: http://www.fishwildlife.org
Facebook: @FishWildlifeAgencies
Twitter: @fishwildlife
This association strives to promote science-based management and conservation of North America's fish and wildlife. Members are mostly American and Canadian.

Canadian Wildlife Federation
350 Michael Cowpland Drive
Kanata, ON K2M 2W1
Canada
(800) 563-9453
Website: http://cwf-fcf.org/en/#
Facebook: @CanadianWildlifeFederation
Twitter and Instagram: @cwf_fcf
This nonprofit organization's mission is to conserve and inspire the conservation of Canada's wildlife and its habitats.

Earth Rangers
9520 Pine Valley Drive
Woodbridge, ON L4H 2Z6
Canada
(905) 417-3447
Website: http://www.earthrangers.org
Facebook: @bringbackthewild
Twitter and Instagram: @EarthRangers
This nonprofit organization dedicated to educating and inspiring children to protect biodiversity and adopt sustainable behaviors.

Environmental Youth Alliance
500-610 Main Street
Vancouver BC V6A 2V3
Canada
(604) 689-4446
Website: http://eya.ca
Facebook: @EnvironmentalYouthAlliance
Twitter: @EnviroYA
This nonprofit charity brings nature experiences to youth in urban areas. They encourage ecological leadership and community connectedness.

Pacific Education Institute
724 Columbia Street NW, Suite 255
Olympia, WA 98501
(360) 705-9294
Website: https://pacificeducationinstitute.org
Facebook: @pacificeducationinstitute
Twitter: @PEIwashington
The institute works toward scientific literacy by empowering educators to teach real-world science outdoors.

Project Learning Tree
c/o Sustainable Forestry Initiative Inc.
2121 K Street, NW, Suite 750
Washington, DC 20037
(202) 765-3641
Website: https://www.plt.org
Facebook: @projectlearningtree
Twitter: @PLT
This environmental education program works with teachers, educators, parents, and community leaders, both in the United States and other countries.

Project WILD
1100 First Street NE, Suite 825
Washington, DC 20002
(713) 520-1936
Website: http://projectwild.org
Project WILD is an environmental education program for kids in kindergarten through high school. Their program focuses on the inherent value of wildlife as a way to teach people about how ecosystems function.

Texas Parks and Wildlife
4200 Smith School Road
Austin, TX 78744
(512) 389-4800
Website: https://tpwd.texas.gov
Facebook: @texasparksandwildlife
Twitter: @TPWDnews
Texas Parks and Wildlife manages and conserves the natural and cultural resources of Texas for present and future generations.

FOR FURTHER READING

Claybourne, Anna. *What Do You Know About Life Cycles?* (Test Your Science Skills). New York, NY: Rosen Publishing, 2018.

Gardner, Robert. *Physics Experiments in Your Own Light Box* (Design, Build, Experiment). New York, NY: Enslow Publishing, 2015.

Heinecke, Liz Lee. *Outdoor Science Lab For Kids: 52 Family-Friendly Experiments for the Yard, Garden, Playground, and Park.* Beverly, MA: Quarry Books, 2016.

Ignotofsky, Rachel. *Women in Science: 50 Fearless Pioneers Who Changed the World.* London, UK: Wren & Rook, 2017.

Krause, Bernard L. *The Great Animal Orchestra: Finding the Origins of Music in the World's Wild Places.* London, UK: Profile, 2013.

Malizia, Diana. *A Visual Guide to Ecology.* New York, NY: Rosen Publishing, 2018.

Mara, Wil. *From Cats' Eyes to ... Reflectors.* Ann Arbor, MI: Cherry Lake Publishing, 2013.

Mooney, Carla, and Samuel Carbaugh. *Chemistry: Investigate the Matter That Makes Up Your World.* White River Junction, VT: Nomad Press, 2016.

Ottaviani, Jim, and Maris Wicks. *Primates: The Fearless Science of Jane Goodall, Dian Fossey, and Biruté Galdikas.* New York, NY: Square Fish, 2015.

Trautmann, Nancy M. *Citizen Science: 15 Lessons That Bring Biology to Life.* Arlington, VA: NSTA Press, National Science Teachers Association, 2013.

Upson, Matt, Colin Michael Hall, and Kevin Cannon. *Information Now: A Graphic Guide to Student Research.* Chicago, IL: The University of Chicago Press, 2015.

VanCleave, Janice Pratt. *Many More of Janice VanCleave's Wild, Wacky, and Weird Physics Experiments.* New York, NY: Rosen Publishing, 2018.

BIBLIOGRAPHY

Biomimicry Institute, "Solutions to Global Challenges Are All Around Us." Retrieved February 16, 2018. https://biomimicry.org/biomimicry-examples.

Brennand, Emma. "Owls Change Colour as Climate Warms." BBC Earth News, February 22, 2011. http://news.bbc.co.uk/earth/hi/earth_news/newsid_9401000/9401733.stm.

Bro-Jørgensen, Jakob. "Overt Female Mate Competition and Preference for Central Males in a Lekking Antelope," National Academy of Sciences, July 2002.

Chandler, David L. "How to Communicate Science Visually." MIT News. October 26, 2012. http://news.mit.edu/2012/communicating-science-visually-felice-frankel-1026.

Crosslin, Rick, and Mary Fortney. "Science Works: Science Is All Around You. Explore, Make a Prediction and Investigate." Children's Museum of Indianapolis. Retrieved February 16, 2018. https://www.childrensmuseum.org.

Goodrich, Ryan. "Who Invented Velcro?" Live Science, May 21, 2013. https://www.livescience.com/34572-velcro.html.

Kids Discover. "Life Science." Retrieved January 5, 2018. https://online.kidsdiscover.com/discover/life-science?utm_source=Pinterest&utm_medium=Ad&utm_campaign=LifeSciencePN&pp=0.

Krause, Bernie. "The Voice of the Natural World," Global TED Talks, June 2013. https://www.ted.com/talks/bernie_krause_the_voice_of_the_natural_world.

Manaugh, Geoff, and Nicola Twilley. "What Did the Continents Look Like Millions of Years Ago?" *The Atlantic*, September 23, 2013. https://www.theatlantic.com/technology/archive/2013/09/what-did-the-continents-look-like-millions-of-years-ago/279892.

National Geographic Society. "Field Investigations." Retrieved January

12, 2018. https://www.nationalgeographic.org/activity/field-investigations.

National Geographic Society. "Mapping Biodiversity." Retrieved January 12, 2018. https://www.nationalgeographic.org/activity/mapping-biodiversity.

Nature Conservancy. "Carbon Calculator." Retrieved January 7, 2018. https://www.nature.org/greenliving/carboncalculator/index.htm.

Petz, Bob. "Ozone, Nitrogen Change the Way Rising CO2 Affects Earth's Water Cycle." NASA Earth Science, July 13, 2009. http://www.ecology.com/2011/09/15/ozone-nitrogen-change-rising-co2.

Sipe, Marion. "What Is Innate and Learned Animal Behavior?" Sciencing, January 30, 2018. https://sciencing.com/innate-learned-animal-behavior-6668264.html.

Stanford School of Medicine. "About Ethograms." Retrieved February 17, 2018. http://web.stanford.edu/~jeromeg/cgi-bin/About%20Ethograms.php.

Tudor, Margaret, and Lynne Ferguson. "Field Investigations: Using Outdoor Environments to Foster Student Learning of Scientific Processes." December 2007. https://tpwd.texas.gov/publications/nonpwdpubs/media/field_investigation_guide.pdf.

University of Texas at Austin. "Field Investigations and Activities." Retrieved December 28, 2017. http://www.gcisd-k12.org/cms/lib/TX01000829/Centricity/Domain/75/Ch_4_Field_Investigations.pdf.

USGS. "Surface Runoff—The Water Cycle," Retrieved February 1, 2018. https://water.usgs.gov/edu/watercyclerunoff.html.

Venton, Danielle. "Mother Nature as Engineer: 9 Design Tricks Borrowed from Biology." *Wired*, August 16, 2011. https://www.wired.com/2011/08/biomimicry-gallery.

INDEX

ABOUT THE AUTHOR

Kristina Lyn Heitkamp is a Utah-based writer, researcher, and environmental journalist. She earned a BA in English from the University of Utah and an MA in environmental science and natural-resource journalism from the University of Montana. She has provided research for several titles with National Geographic Books and has authored nonfiction books and articles on various topics, including soundscape ecology and bison conservation. When Heitkamp is not writing about our relationship with the environment, she is pestering her sister, a wildlife ecologist, for details about her latest field investigation.

PHOTO CREDITS

Cover, pp. 1, 23 Hero Images/Getty Images; p. 3 Ollyy/Shutterstock.com; p. 4 Pressmaster/Shutterstock.com; p. 5 Courtesy Raymond M. Alf Museum of Paleontology; p. 10 Sarah2/Shutterstock.com; p. 13 Designua /Shutterstock.com; p. 15 Aleksandr Borovikov/Shutterstock.com; p. 17 © Monika Halinowska/Moment/Getty Images; p. 20 Greg Vaughn /Alamy Stock Photo; p. 25 Merlin Halteman/Shutterstock.com; p. 28 Michael Nichols/NATIONAL GEOGRAPHIC IMAGE COLLECTION /Getty Images; p. 30 Daniel Koebe/Corbis/VCG/Getty Images; p. 33 Terence/Shutterstock.com; p. 36 Anton Foltin/Shutterstock.com; p. 37 TCreativeMedia/Shutterstock.com; p. 41 Fuse/Corbis/Getty Images; p. 44 Spencer Sutton/Science Source; p. 46 Joe Petersburger/National Geographic Magazines/Getty Images; p. 48 Monkey Business Images/Shutterstock.com; p. 51 (left) Alexey Seafarer/Shutterstock.com, (right) critterbiz/Shutterstock .com; p. 53 Image by Catherine MacBride/Moment/Getty Images.

Design: Nelson Sá; Layout: Ellina Litmanovich; Editor: Amelie von Zumbusch; Photo Researcher: Nicole DiMella